IP SUBNET BEGINNERS

NOVICE TO PRO GUIDE TO UNDERSTANDING SUBNETTING WITH STEP BY STEP GUIDE AND DIAGRAMS

Mac Andrews

TABLE OF CONTENT

CHAPTER 1
IPv4 DEFINITION

The Internet Protocol or IP was developed during the 1980's and was designed to work with 32 bits data to define an IP address i.e. 192.168.1.1. to briefly explain bits with the previous example, 192.168.1.1 contains 4 fields that are separated by a dot. Each of the fields can have an allocation of 8 bits of data. 8 bits * 4 fields = 32 bits.

The maximum number of IPv4 addresses is 4.3 Billion while the number of devices connected to the internet as of 2016 is 20 billion. This means the number of available addresses has by far been outnumbered by devices but this does not mean the devices cannot be connected to the internet. A number of measures have been put in place to slow IPv4 address allocation with the use of technology such as NAT in addition to the introduction of public and private IP. IPv6 protocol has also been introduced which is a far better strategy.

IPv4 CLASSES

As earlier stated, each field in an IPv4 can have values between 0-255 which is 8bits per field. Therefore 256 values, 2 ^ 8=256. IP addresses are divided into classes

IP Class	Start IP	End IP	Network Prefix
A	1.0.0.0	127.255.255.255	1-27
B	128.0.0.0	191.255.255.255	128-191
C	190.0.0.0	223.255.255.255	192-223
D	224.0.0.0	239.255.255.255	224-239
E	240.0.0.0	255.255.255.255	240-255

The ones used on the internet are classes A, B, and C. Class D is reserved for Multicast addresses while class E is not being used because of its an experimental class.

PUBLIC IP AND PRIVATE IP

Public IP as the name implies transmits information publicly via the internet while Private IP is used in the LAN or Local Area Network which is found in our Schools, Offices or Homes.

The private Ip address does not reach the internet. This is why NAT was created to enable Private IP to communicate over the internet. The NAT transforms Private IP's into Public IP's.

PRIVATE IP ADDRESSES

The below table informs on the ranges of Private IP addresses:

IP Class	Start IP	IP End	Network Profile
A	10.0.0.1	10.255.255.255	10.0.0.0/8
B	172.16.0.1	172.31.255.255	172.16.0.0/12
C	192.168.0.1	192.168.255.255	192.168.0.0/16

The IP addresses not found in the above table are public

We can similarly have the above scenario below with multiple LANs Network A and S containing both Private and Public IP for the remaining networks.

With the help of NAT, private IP addresses ensure improved network security which makes it very secure against attackers.

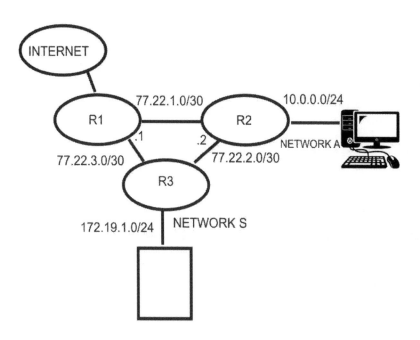

INTERNET

77.22.1.0/30

R1

R2

10.0.0.0/24

.1 .2

77.22.3.0/30 77.22.2.0/30

NETWORK A

R3

172.19.1.0/24 NETWORK S

CHAPTER 2
IPV4 PACKET STRUCTURE

8		8	8	8
Version	Header Length	Type of Service or Diff Serv	Total Length	
Identifyer			Flags	Fragment Offset
Time to Live		Protocol	Header Checksum	
Source Address				
Destination Address				
Options			Padding	

32 Bits

From the above, there are important components that we will come across in the tech career

- IP Destination Address
- IP Source Address
- ToS (Type of Service)
- TTL (Time to Live)
- Header Checksum

Each will briefly be discussed in detail starting with IP addresses. You must know by now that a source address and destination address are required for communication between two devices. The source address field and destination address field are reserved for the source IP address and destination IP address.

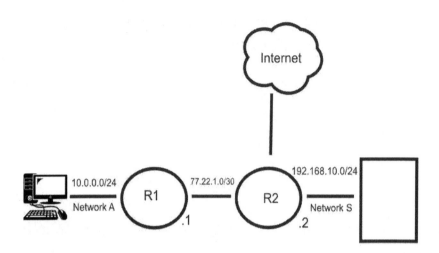

Network A 10.0.0.0/24   R1   77.22.1.0/30   R2   192.168.10.0/24   Network S

NETWORK LOOP PREVENTION WITH TTL

There is a really important component right within the IP header called TTL (Time to Live). This serves as a mechanism to protect against Network Loops that may happen in connection between Routers or on the internet.

255 is the value of each TTL by default for each packet although it can have a value between 1-255. On every loop, the value decreases when it reaches another router or network. taking from fig 1.3, when a packet is sent from the PC to the S server, the packets:

- Get to R1 with its value at 255
- R1, in turn, sends to R2 with an updated value of 254
- The packet finally reaches S server with value 253

If there was a misconfiguration on R2, it would think R1 is connected directly to the server. This would create a network loop for R2 because it will send packets back to R1 and R1 would send back to R2 also thinking the server is on R2.

This loop will continue till the Routers CPU reach 100% workload and network slow down causing downtime indefinitely if the TTL did not exist.

If the TTL value equals 0, the router receiving the packets will drop it

```
C:\Users\sijugk>ping yahoo.com

Pinging yahoo.com [98.139.183.24] with 32 bytes of data:
Reply from 98.139.183.24: bytes=32 time=370ms TTL=39
Reply from 98.139.183.24: bytes=32 time=486ms TTL=38
Reply from 98.139.183.24: bytes=32 time=392ms TTL=38
Reply from 98.139.183.24: bytes=32 time=698ms TTL=38

Ping statistics for 98.139.183.24:
    Packets: Sent = 4, Received = 4, Lost = 0 (0% loss),
Approximate round trip times in milli-seconds:
    Minimum = 370ms, Maximum = 698ms, Average = 486ms

C:\Users\sijugk>ping Google.com

Pinging google.com [74.125.236.165] with 32 bytes of data:
Reply from 74.125.236.165: bytes=32 time=85ms TTL=52
Reply from 74.125.236.165: bytes=32 time=80ms TTL=52
Reply from 74.125.236.165: bytes=32 time=95ms TTL=52
Reply from 74.125.236.165: bytes=32 time=90ms TTL=52

Ping statistics for 74.125.236.165:
    Packets: Sent = 4, Received = 4, Lost = 0 (0% loss),
Approximate round trip times in milli-seconds:
    Minimum = 80ms, Maximum = 95ms, Average = 87ms

C:\Users\sijugk>ping corenetworkz.com

Pinging corenetworkz.com [192.64.119.167] with 32 bytes of data:
Reply from 192.64.119.167: bytes=32 time=384ms TTL=43
Reply from 192.64.119.167: bytes=32 time=420ms TTL=43
Reply from 192.64.119.167: bytes=32 time=376ms TTL=43
Reply from 192.64.119.167: bytes=32 time=371ms TTL=43
```

VERSION, ToS and header checksum

VERSION
IP protocol comes in two versions

1. IP version 4
2. IP version 6

ToS (TYPE OF SERVICE)
This is a very important element in QoS (Quality of Service). This field marks a package that needs to be treated a special way (priority / VIP access)

QoS ensures service quality in real-time applications.

HEADER CHECKSUM
A packet's checksum helps maintain its integrity. We want a situation where whatever we send, reaches its destination. There is a loss of packet or altered information when we send data over the internet. Checksum ensures the integrity of this information.

It's basically a mathematical formula that generates a unique ID for all packets introduced to the formula. Therefore, when a source is about to send packets to a destination, each packet is passed through the formula and has its value added to the Header Checksum field in IPv4.

Once the packets have arrived its destination, the IDs of each packet are recalculated individually. The integrity is said to have been maintained if the value for the sent is the same as received.

Other IP header elements include:

- Total Length (of the header in bytes)
- Flags / Fragments Offset (if fragmentation is required for packet
- Options (an additional option for I packets although rarely used)
- Protocol (specifies the protocol being used. UDP or TCP)
- Identifier (identifier of IP packet
- Padding (adjusts the packet length to ensure it's a multiple of 32 (bits)

CHAPTER 3
IP SUBNETTING

This is a very important design and functionality of computer network which if not properly and efficiently implemented, will lead to high cost and low performance of the network. 32 bits make up the address of an IPv4. IPv4 contains 4 fields with capacity of 8 bits each. There is a potential value of 0-255 for each field making 256 in total possible values. With the 8 bits, $2^8=256$. See the example below.

192.168.0.0/24

192.168.0.0 is the network address or see it as the name of a street for instance.

/24 is the network mask which can be seen as the maximum number of houses in a street.

Network mask has a function of determining the network size which is the total amount of IP addresses that make up the network.

Parts of IP address:

1. Network portion – its size is in bits and is dictated by the network mask
2. Host portion – the bits that remain out of the 32 bits

For example, the IP address 192.168.0.0/24 is a network address just like the street name

/24 representing the mask which means the first 24 bits represent the network portion while the 8 bits remaining represents the host portion.

Therefore, if we are to allocate IP addresses on 192.168.0.0, the first3 fields will remain unchanged (192.168.0) the last remaining field can then be used to identify devices which can range from .1 to .254. example below:

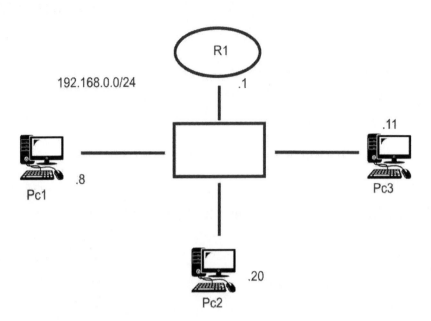

Example: 3 devices to assign an IP address from 192.168.0.0/24

Device 1: 192.168.0.8

Device 2: 192.168.0.11

Device 3: 192.168.0.20

Normally, the router has the first or last IP address in the network which would either be 192.168.0.1 or 192.168.0.254.

Therefore, the IP address for R1 will be 192.168.0.1

IP SUBNETTING GUIDE

This is a technique that allows the allocation of a certain amount of IP addresses for networks to accomplish specific goals. Let's take some time to do a little exercise.

1. what is the number of IP addresses we can generate from a defined mask? In this case /24
2. what is the first and last IP address?
3. Which IP address can be used from the network?

E.g. 1

For instance, 192.168.0.0/24 will be used for No 3

1. $32 - 24 = 8$, $2^8=256$ which is the maximum number of IP addresses from network mask /24
2. First IP is 192.168.0.1 while the last is 192.168.0.254
3. All IP addresses from 192.168.0.1 to 192.168.0.254 are useable within the network

192.168.0.0/24 contains the following IP addresses

192.168.0.1, 192.168.0.2, ... 192.168.0.255.

The last IP being 192.168.0.255 cannot be used because it is the broadcast address that is used to reach all devices within the network.

Out of 256, 254 IP addresses will be available because 192.168.0.0 and 192.168.0.255 are unavailable. The first is used to identify the network while the last is used to send traffic to all devices.

E.g. 2

Using 10.222.24.0/24 to answer the same 3 questions

1. 32-24=8, 2^8=256 which is maximum IP addresses from network mask /24
2. First IP is 10.222.24.1 and the last IP is 10.222.24.255
3. Useable addresses in the network are 10.222.24.1-10.222.24.254

E.g. 3

Using 172.22.9.0/27 to answer the same 3 questions

1. 32-27=5, 2^5=32 which is maximum IP addresses from network mask /27
2. First IP is 172.22.9.1 and the last IP is 172.22.9.31
3. Useable addresses in the network are 172.22.9.1-17222.9.30

E.g. 4

Using 192.168.11.0/30 to answer the same 3 questions

1. 32-30=2, 2^2=4 which is maximum IP addresses from network mask /24

2. First IP is 192.168.11.1 and the last IP is 192.168.11.3
3. Useable addresses in the network are 192.168.11.1-192.168.11.2

THE NEXT NETWORK

In subnetting, the current network isn't our only point of interest but also the next network. for instance:

192.168.0.0/27

32-27=5, 2^5=32. 32 is the total number of IP addresses from network mask /27. It also shows the delimitation between networks

Based on this principle, the next network will be:

192.168.0.32/27, then

192.168.0.64/27

192.168.0.96/27

192.168.0.128/27

This means there is an increment of 32 for the network mask/27.

Examples below:

Network IP	First IP	Last IP	Next IP
192.168.0.0/24	192.168.0.1	192.168.0.255	192.168.1.0/24
10.0.0.0/27	10.0.0.1	10.0.0.31	10.0.0.32/27
10.10.0.128/26	10.10.0.129	10.10.0.191	10.10.0.192/26

If we have a mask of /24, the total number of IP addresses is 256. The number of IP addresses must be between 0-255. We cannot have the number 256. Instead, we move it to the next network. so instead of ~~192.168.0.256,~~ we will have 192.168.1.0.

IP SUBNETTING BASED ON NUMBER OF DEVICES

Let's assume that after reading this book ensure you received an offer to design the network of a firm. This business has 3 departments: Sales, Marketing and IT.

Each of these departments will have certain devices (Laptops, Printers, Servers, etc.) that require an IP address to communicate with each other and the Internet.

Suppose we need 15 IP addresses for Sales, 7 for Marketing, 129 for IT and the available address space is the following: 10.23.0.0/16

This addressing space will contain the following:

1) /16 => 32 - 16 = 16, 2^16 = 65536 IP addresses

2) First IP: 10.23.0.1, Last IP: 10.23.255.255 (Broadcast)

3) All of the following IP addresses 10.23.0.1 - 10.23.255.254 are usable within the network.

Think of each IP address as costing $1 /month. Our goal (with subnetting) is to use as few IP addresses as possible, in order to reduce our costs. If we don't think/do it this way, we risk paying $65,536 / month only for the IPs!

Thus, we'll always start subnetting with the biggest network (based on the total number of IP addresses/devices required):

1. 129 - IT

2. 15 - Sales

3. 7 - Marketing

Now, let's answer these questions:

1) What's the netmask? - ex: /24

2) What's the IP address of the network?

3) How many IP addresses are usable?

4) What's the IP address of the next network?

In order to find the netmask for each network, we must first ask ourselves: "Which is the closest power of 2, greater than the number of devices?"

To find the netmask of each network, we need to first ascertain the closest power of 2 greater than the number of devices?

2^8	2^7	2^6	2^5	2^4	2^3	2^2	2^1	2^0
256	128	64	32	16	8	4	2	1

For example, in the case of the IT department, for 129 (the number of devices in the network) the closest power of 2 will be 8: 2^8 = 256.

As I said before, 256 represents the maximum number of IP addresses, but we can't use all of them. The reason being: the first (.0) address is reserved for the network, and the last (.255) address is reserved for Broadcast.

So, we have to drop 2 IP addresses out of the total 256. Thus, the result will be 256 - 2 = 254. 254 will represent the total number of usable IP addresses.

Now we'll answer the above questions and also find the netmask number.

First, we'll take the number (8) from the power of 2 and do:

1) 32 - 8 = 24 => /24 represents the netmask

2) The network will be 10.23.0.0/24 (the difference between this network and the other one is the network mask - this one, with the /24, is much smaller)

3) The following IP addresses: 10.23.0.1 - 10.23.0.254, are included in the network

4) The next network: 10.23.1.0/24 (out of which we'll continue subnetting) So, the 1st network is: 10.23.0.0/24

In case of the Sales department, $2^5 = 32$ (actually is 32 - 2 = 30) is the closest value to 15 (the number of required IP addresses). We'll also take the power of 2 (which is 5) in order to find the netmask and also answer the

other questions:

1) 32 - 5 = 27 => /27 represents the netmask

2) The network is 10.23.1.0/27

3) The following IP addresses: 10.23.1.1 - 10.23.1.30, are included in the network

4) The next network: 10.23.1.32/27 (out of which we'll continue subnetting)

The 2nd network is: 10.23.1.0/27

In case of the Marketing department, $2^4 = 16$ (actually is 16 - 2 = 14) is the closest value to 7 (the number of required IP addresses):

And here are the answers for the 4 questions:

1) 32 - 4 = 28 => /28 represents the netmask

2) The network is 10.23.1.32/28

3) The following IP addresses: 10.23.1.33 - 10.23.1.46 are included in the network

4) The next network: 10.23.1.48/28

So, the 3rd network is: 10.23.1.32/28

CHAPTER 4
HOW TO CONFIGURE IP ADDRESS ON WINDOWS 7/8/10

Let's configure an IP address on PC with a Cisco Router

192.168.1.0/24

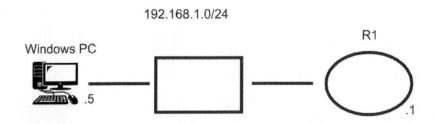

There are two options to set up an IP address on windows which could either be from the GUI or Command-Line. Lets, first of all, check the IP address via command line.

```
Microsoft Windows [Version 6.1.7601]
Copyright (c) 2009 Microsoft Corporation. All rights reserved.

C:\Users\oracle>ipconfig

Windows IP Configuration


Ethernet adapter Local Area Connection 2:

    Connection-specific DNS Suffix  . :
    Link-local IPv6 Address . . . . . : fe80::80e7:3223:ac5c:39e9%16
    IPv4 Address. . . . . . . . . . . : 192.168.1.170
    Subnet Mask . . . . . . . . . . . : 255.255.255.0
    Default Gateway . . . . . . . . . : 192.168.1.2

Ethernet adapter Bluetooth Network Connection:

    Media State . . . . . . . . . . . : Media disconnected
    Connection-specific DNS Suffix  . :

Tunnel adapter isatap.{EDB96DF3-34AA-41A1-8809-9B27B2DF11B3}:

    Media State . . . . . . . . . . . : Media disconnected
    Connection-specific DNS Suffix  . :
```

Type ipconfig followed by the enter key when the command is open. Information regarding your PC's network configuration will be displayed which includes Bluetooth, Wi-Fi, Ethernet adapters. Vital information shown includes:

- Network Mask
- IPv4 Address
- Default Gateway
- IPv6 Address

We can configure all of these with one of two methods which are:

Dynamically – DHCP a protocol configured on the server and assign dynamically. This means the IP will be assigned without human interaction

Statically – here the information is manually inputted

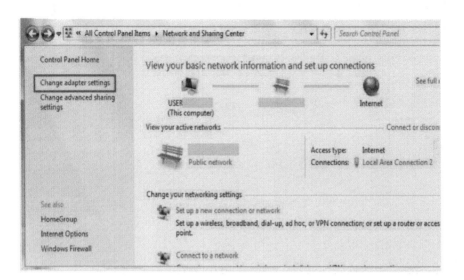

To configure static IP, go to Control Panel> (Network and Sharing Center> Change adapter settings) or (Network and Internet> Network connections)

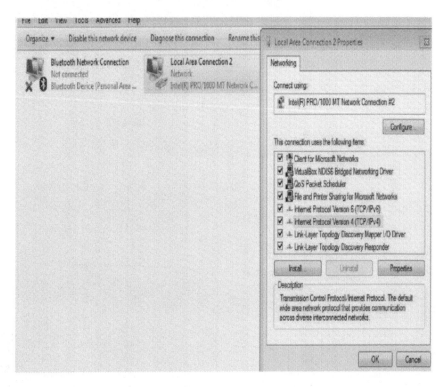

Right-click on "Local Area Connection" and select "Properties". From the new window that opens, select IPv4 and click Properties. The next figure will enable you to configure the IP Address, Subnet Mask, Default Gateway and DNS Server.

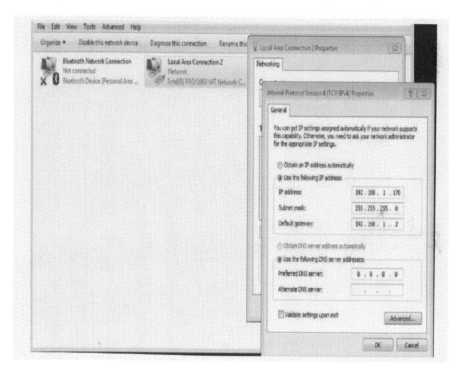

For example, let us choose a network like 192.168.1.0/24. The PC will be assigned 192.168.1.170. the /24 in decimal mask looks 255.255.255.0 and the default gateway which is the internet-connected router will be 192.168.1.2.

We need to configure the DNS server which will help with name resolution from a domain and will provide us with an IP address like 216.58.214.227. the DNS IP is 8.8.8.8

Now go to CMD with the below commands:

```
>ping 8.8.8.8              //checks the internet
connection

>ping google.ro           //checks the DNS service
and internet connection

>nslookup google.ro       //checks the DNS service
```

CHAPTER 5
HOW TO CONFIGURE IP ADDRESS ON ROUTER

Let's configure an IP address on Cisco router R1. A router basically interconnects more than one network via ports. Port is a physical place you can plug a cable while the part of a port that is logical is called an interface.

Port = Physical

Interface = Logical

For example, we can set up an IP being a logical address on an interface and physically connect the cable to a port.

The interfaces need to have an IP address configured in order to communicate within the network and the interface needs to be turned on. See how to set up an IP address on an interface below.

R1(config)#interface FastEthernet0/0

R1(config-if)#ip address 192.168.1.1 255.255.255.0

R1(config-if)#no shutdown

With this, you have a working network and can further connect to the internet and communicate with devices connected to the same network.

IPv6

There are over 20 billion devices and counting connected to the internet all over the world. This is a problem for ISPs (Internet Service Providers) because this figure is far more than the estimated and anticipated 4.3 billion IPv4 was providing.

There is an urgent need for a larger protocol and this is where IPv6 plays a key role. This is a new addressing protocol that has a new format which is hexadecimal. There is a much larger address space with 128 bits which means 2^{128} addresses are available.

IPv6 looks like:

2003:4581:A7C1:EFDB:0000:0000:1327:0001

The above address is very much different from IPv4. The IPv6 forms out of Hexa characters which comprise of 16 values between A-F and 0-9

SIMPLIFYING IPv6 ADDRESS

It was observed the addresses were too long and so it was decided that the address should be simplified as below:

1. When 2 or more fields consecutively have 0s, (0000:0000)
   You can reduce it to

1234:ABCD:3123:0000:0000:0000:0000   =
1234:ABCD:3123::

Example, the IPv6 default route looks like, ::/0 which is shorter than IPv4 which is 0.0.0.0/0

2. When there aren't consecutive fields with 0s, a group of 0s (0000) could be written as 0.
1234:ABCD:3123:00A8:0A31:8000:0000:0001   =
1234:ABCD:3123:00A8:0A31:8000:0:0001

3. We can further simplify the above example:
1234:ABCD:3123:00A8:0A31:8000:0000:0001   =
1234:ABCD:3123:A8:A31:8000:0:1
The 0s have been eliminated.
00A8=A8 0001=1

E.g.   2003:4581:A7C1:EFDB:0000:0000:1327:0001   =
2003:4581:A7C1:EFDB::1327:1

ADDRESS TYPES FOR IPv6

There are two types of IPv6 addresses namely, Global (2000::/3 used on the internet) and Local Link Address (FE80::/10 used in LANs)

IPv6 GLOBAL ADDRESSES

This is similar to public IPv4 addresses because they cannot just be used in LAN but on the internet too. These global addresses always start with 2 or 3 because their subnet mask is 2000::/3

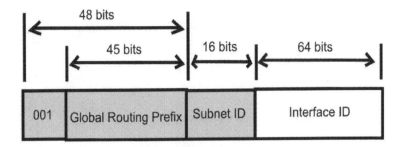

The first 3 bits are reserved and this is the reason IPv6 global addresses start with 2. Next, the global routing prefix which is the addressing space reserved for ISP. The network ID is represented by the subnet ID (total of 65536 = 2^16). The last field is the interface ID which is the IPv6 address of the device. Some examples are below:

- 3731:ADE0:9923:23::90/64
- 2001:DB8:A0B:12F0::1/64
- 2020:ABCD:1:FFF0:84:ADEF/64

IPv6 LINK-LOCAL ADDRESS

Special addresses exist that make communication among devices within a network possible. These addresses are usually configured automatically (auto-config) and need no user intervention.

The format of Link-Local IPv6 addresses are FE80::/10. They begin with FE80 while the remaining address is auto-generated bu EUI-64. For instance, if you look at CMD on a Windows PC you can see IPv6 Link-Local Address

The Link-Local address of the Ethernet interface is represented by the first IPv6 address while the second which starts with 2001:0... belong to the tunnel interface and is the global IPv6 address.

The EUI-64 technique is used to generate the Link-Local address which is used by many vendors like Juniper, Cisco, Linux, etc. unlike these vendors, Microsoft generates the Ipv6Link-Local address randomly for windows.

EUI-64 technique uses the MAC addresses and an FFFE Hexa field to form IPv6 Link-Local address.

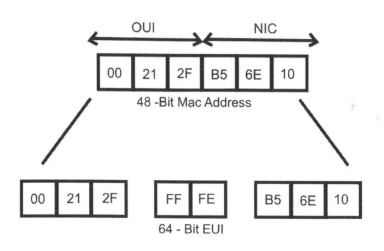

The initial MAC address 00:21:2F:B5:6E:10 is separated into 2 parts and in the middle the FF:FE values are being added. Thus, 0021:2FFF:FEB5:6E10

will represent the host bits of the newly generated IPv6 address: FE80::0021:2FFF:FEB5:6E10/64

In some cases, the 2nd bit (of the added string) is switched (1 -> 0 or 0 -> 1).

In this scenario, our IPv6 address will look similar to:

FE80::0021:2FFF:FEB5:6E10/64   =
FE80::0023:2FFF:FEB5:6E10/64

TRANSMITTING PACKETS IN 3 WAYS

There isn't BROADCAST in IPv6 like the IPv4, what we have is Multicast.

IPv6 traffic can be sent via

- Unicast – one on one
- Anycast- one to closest
- Multicast – One to many

An example of Anycast traffic is if we want to go to a website like google.com for instance, the name will be translated into an IP address with a DNS server. There are multiple DNS servers in the US and the message will simply be sent to the closest server which will reduce the browsing wait time and make it appear the browsing experience is fast.

IPv6 SUBNETTING

In the IPv6 network, there are enough addresses to go around and you need not worry about that. There are /64, /80, /96and other masks. Using /64, let's see what it looks like.

2002:ABCD:1234:9FD8::/64

In the above case, the first 64 bits which are the first 4 fields do not change but remain the same.

So, we can assign a mask of /80 for any network we want. Let's assume that we need 4 networks, each with a different number of IP addresses that are required (all fitting into /80).

1st network: 2002:ABCD:1234:9FD8:0000::/80 (or 2002:ABCD:1234:9FD8::/80)

2nd network: 2002:ABCD:1234:9FD8:0001::/80 (or 2002:ABCD:1234:9FD8:1::/80)

3rd network: 2002:ABCD:1234:9FD8:0002::/80 (or 2002:ABCD:1234:9FD8:2::/80)

4th network: 2002:ABCD:1234:9FD8:0003::/80 (or 2002:ABCD:1234:9FD8:3::/80)

What did I do above? I carefully looked in what field I was in (5th out of 8) and I added 1 from one network to the other).

It doesn't make any sense to overstress with subnetting based on how many IP addresses we need in our networks. All we have to do is use the IPv6 address space provided to us by our ISPs and break it down into smaller networks (with a mask of /64, /80, /89, etc.).

After that, we'll ask ourselves: "how many networks do I need?". And after that, we'll start dividing the big network (provided by our ISP) into smaller ones.

In other words, if we receive a /64 network, then we'll use /80 for our smaller ones.

HOW TO USE IPv4 AND IPv6 PROTOCOLS ON THE INTERNET

There are times we might have in the same network, devices that are configured in IPv6 while others configured in IPv4. These devices cannot communicate and as such, we have some ways to solve this issue.

- DUAL STACK
- 6to4 or 4to6 Tunnel
- NAT-PT (NAT64)

DUAL STACK

This is very simple. You only have to configure both v6 and v4 addresses on the device and the device will communicate effectively with any device in the network.

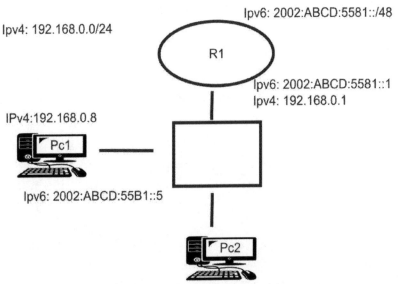

Ipv6: 2002:ABCD:5581::/48

Ipv4: 192.168.0.0/24

Ipv6: 2002:ABCD:5581::1
Ipv4: 192.168.0.1

IPv4:192.168.0.8

Ipv6: 2002:ABCD:55B1::5

Ipv4: 192.168.0.20   Ipv6: 2002:ABCD:5581::41

6TO4 OR 4TO6 TUNNELS

In a scenario where 2 IPv6 networks are connected to 2 routers in separate geographical regions and connected by a large IPv4 network. The PCs connected to the 2 networks can't communicate with each other because of the incompatibility of IPv4 and IPv6.

To solve this, create a 6to4 tunnel between the routers which can then transport the IPv6 addresses over the IPv4 network.

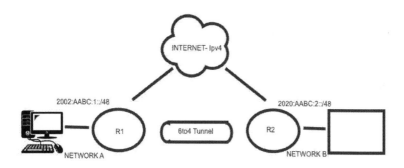

NAT-PT (Network Address Translation -Protocol Translation)

Recall the NAT (Network Address Translation) is used to translate Private IP Address to Public IP Address by the router to allow the device access to the internet.

The NAT-PT basically does the same. The only difference is that it converts IPv4 address to IPv6 and vice versa.

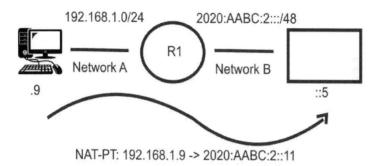

HOW TO CONFIGURE IPv6

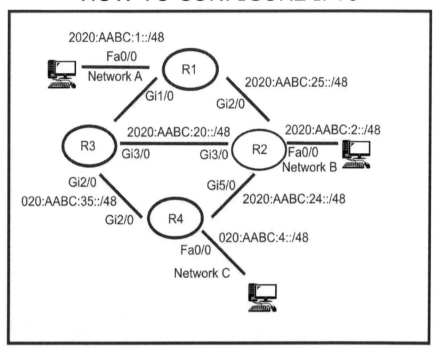

Normally, the PC's IPv6 address does not need to be configured because it has an auto-configuration feature. There are some situations a manual/static address for instance if there is a server on the windows machine. Follow the below steps to configure windows:

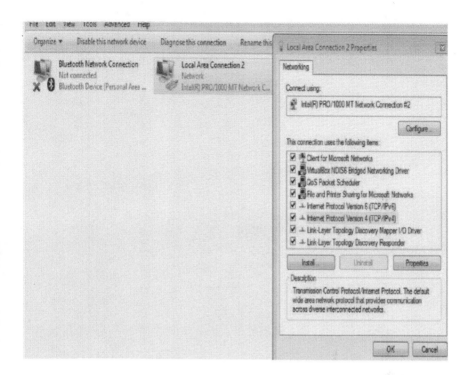

From here, we select IPv6 and click on properties. The next windows allow you to insert an IPv6 address, a default gateway, a netmask, and DNS server.

Below are the IPv6 settings:

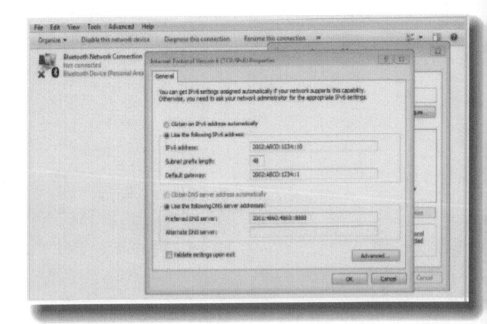

Let's check the configuration done above >ipconfig

```
C:\Users\oracle>ipconfig

Windows IP Configuration

Ethernet adapter Local Area Connection 2:

   Connection-specific DNS Suffix  . :
   IPv6 Address. . . . . . . . . . . : 2002:abcd:1234::10
   Link-local IPv6 Address . . . . . : fe80::8067:2223:ac5e:39e9x16
   IPv4 Address. . . . . . . . . . . : 192.168.1.170
   Subnet Mask . . . . . . . . . . . : 255.255.255.0
   Default Gateway . . . . . . . . . : 2002:abcd:1234::1
                                       192.168.1.2

Ethernet adapter Bluetooth Network Connection:

   Media State . . . . . . . . . . . : Media disconnected
   Connection-specific DNS Suffix  . :

Tunnel adapter isatap.{EDD96DF3-34AA-41A1-8809-9B27B2DP11B3}:

   Media State . . . . . . . . . . . : Media disconnected
   Connection-specific DNS Suffix  . :
```

Now, after we saw how to set an IPv6 address on Windows, it's time to move further and see how can we do it on a professional networking equipment (in this case a Cisco Router):

On R1 the config will be:

R1(config)#ipv6 unicast-routing

R1(config)#interface Fa0/0

R1(config-if)#ipv6 address 2020:AABC:1::1/48

R1(config-if)#no shutdown

R1(config)#interface Gi1/0

R1(config-if)#ipv6 address 2020:AABC:15::1/48

R1(config-if)#no shutdown

R1(config)#interface Gi2/0

R1(config-if)#ipv6 address 2020:AABC:25::1/48

R1(config-if)#no shutdown

```
R1(config)#
R1(config)#ipv6 unicast-routing
R1(config)#interface fa0/0
R1(config-if)#ipv6 address 2020:AABC:1::1/48
R1(config-if)#exit
R1(config)#interface Gi1/0
R1(config-if)#ipv6 address 2020:AABC:15::1/48
R1(config-if)#exit
R1(config)#interface Gi2/0
R1(config-if)#ipv6 address 2020:AABC:25::1/48
R1(config-if)#exit
R1(config)#
```

On R2 the config will be:

R2(config)#ipv6 unicast-routing

R2(config)#interface Gi1/0

R2(config-if)#ipv6 address 2020:AABC:15::2/48

R2(config-if)#no shutdown

R2(config)#interface Gi2/0

R2(config-if)#ipv6 address 2020:AABC:35::1/48

R2(config-if)#no shutdown

R2(config)#interface Gi3/0

R2(config-if)#ipv6 address 2020:AABC:20::1/48

R2(config-if)#no shutdown

```
R2#
R2#conf t
Enter configuration commands, one per line.  End with CNTL/Z.
R2(config)#ipv6 unicast-routing
R2(config)#interface Gi1/0
R2(config-if)#ipv6 address 2020:AABC:18::2/48
R2(config-if)#exit
R2(config)#interface Gi2/0
R2(config-if)#ipv6 address 2020:AABC:98::1/48
R2(config-if)#exit
R2(config)#interface Gi3/0
R2(config-if)#ipv6 address 2020:AABC:20::1/48
R2(config-if)#exit
R2(config)#
```

On R3 the config will be:

R3(config)#ipv6 unicast-routing

R3(config)#interface Fa0/0

R3(config-if)#ipv6 address 2020:AABC:2::1/48

R3(config-if)#no shutdown

R3(config)#interface Gi2/0

R3(config-if)#ipv6 address 2020:AABC:25::2/48

R3(config-if)#no shutdown

R3(config)#interface Gi3/0

R3(config-if)#ipv6 address 2020:AABC:20::2/48

R3(config-if)#no shutdown

R3(config)#interface Gi5/0

R3(config-if)#ipv6 address 2020:AABC:24::1/48

R3(config-if)#no shutdown

```
R3#
R3#conf t
Enter configuration commands, one per line.  End with CNTL/Z.
R3(config)#ipv6 unicast-routing
R3(config)#interface fa0/0
R3(config-if)#ipv6 address 2020:AABC:2::1/48
R3(config-if)#exit
R3(config)#interface Gi2/0
R3(config-if)#ipv6 address 2020:AABC:25::2/48
R3(config-if)#exit
R3(config)#interface Gi3/0
R3(config-if)#ipv6 address 2020:AABC:20::2/48
R3(config-if)#exit
R3(config)#interface Gi5/0
R3(config-if)#ipv6 address 2020:AABC:26::1/48
R3(config-if)#exit
R3(config)#
```

On R4 the config will be:

R4(config)#ipv6 unicast-routing

R4(config)#interface Fa0/0

R4(config-if)#ipv6 address 2020:AABC:4::1/48

R4(config-if)#no shutdown

R4(config)#interface Gi2/0

R4(config-if)#ipv6 address 2020:AABC:35::2/48

R4(config-if)#no shutdown

R4(config)#interface Gi5/0

R4(config-if)#ipv6 address 2020:AABC:24::2/48

R4(config-if)#no shutdown

```
R4#
R4#conf t
Enter configuration commands, one per line.  End with CNTL/Z.
R4(config)#ipv6 unicast-routing
R4(config)#interface Fa0/0
R4(config-if)#ipv6 address 2020:AABC:4::1/48
R4(config-if)#exit
R4(config)#interface Gi2/0
R4(config-if)#ipv6 address 2020:AABC:35::2/48
R4(config-if)#exit
R4(config)#interface Gi5/0
R4(config-if)#ipv6 address 2020:AABC:24::2/48
R4(config-if)#exit
R4(config)#
```

The IPv6 address has successfully been configured on the routers

Made in the USA
Middletown, DE
27 February 2020